SCHIRMER'S LIBRARY
OF MUSICAL CLASSICS

Vol. 15

Johann Sebastian Bach

Short Preludes and Fugues

For the Pianoforte

Edited and Fingered by
DR. WM. MASON

G. SCHIRMER, Inc.

DISTRIBUTED BY
HAL•LEONARD®
CORPORATION
7777 W. BLUEMOUND RD. P.O. BOX 13819 MILWAUKEE, WI 53213

CONTENTS.

PREFACE.

The titles of these compositions are a sufficient evidence of our purpose to collect the easiest instructive works of J. S. Bach in a single volume. They are given, in part, in accordance with the author's own manuscripts; in part (where the latter were lacking) after the best early copies.

When the autograph was at hand it was followed implicitly, as is proper; for any variants found in copies do not indicate later improvements on the master's part, but are mere mistakes in writing, or arbitrary "corrections," unworthy of notice. During the work of restoring the other pieces, of which no original autographs exist, and which could be written out only by collating several old copies, we were guided by the most scrupulous conscientiousness and, in case of frequent conflicting readings, by a most careful study of Bach's style and art, so that we may hope that a connoisseur may hardly be found who will refuse his approval of our final decisions.

As to the signs employed for the embellishments, and their execution, they are to be understood thus:

the sign ᷈ is written instead of *tr*, when the after-beat is written out; *e.g.*, ; otherwise the same sign ᷈ calls for a trill without after-beat; but in this case the last trill-beat must be played quicker than the others. Every trill on a dotted note closes, when the after-beat is not written out, on the dot, and the short note following the dot retains its entire time-value. The Bach trill, to be properly executed, must never be begun on the note over which the sign stands, but on the next note above, either a tone or a semitone higher, according to the scale. Bach considered the trill as a manifold repetition of the appoggiatura, and regarded its æsthetic charm as lying in the repeated alternation of a suspension with its resolution; this also explains the function of the after-beat, without which final satisfaction could not be attained. Should the auxiliary trill-tone be foreign to the key in which the piece is written, it has a special chromatic sign. The occasional sign (᷈ or (᷈ is explained by J. S. Bach himself, in the "Clavierbuchlein" for W. F. Bach, as follows:

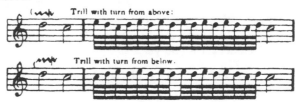

(N.B.—For the convenience of students, the embellishments are, in this edition, written out in full in small notes.)

With regard to the marks of tempo and expression which we have added, only tradition, as handed down to men still living, could decide. Its authenticity will not be doubted after the statement is made, that the principal medium for its conveyance was Forkel, whom Wilhelm Friedemann and C. Ph. Em. Bach recognized as a true disciple of the Bach school.

It may seem strange, that marking by means of slurs and dots over the notes is generally omitted. The reason is found in the nature of the case. It was feared that slurs might induce a "sticky" style, and dots a too detached style, in executing the melodies. Either would be foreign to the true interpretation of Bach's clavier-compositions, according to which the tones should be like a string of pearls, each touching the next at one point only. It would be far better to hold the individual phrases together by slurs, and to indicate by dots the places where one phrase ends and another commences. Some such punctuation is necessary for piano-players of the present time, when they are to play Bach's compositions; for the proper phrasing of the latter is not a matter of course to them. An attempt to use slurs and dots in this way has been made most fully in No. 9 of the Twelve little Preludes for Beginners. Old-time players understood this style of playing thoroughly, and introduced great animation into their phrasing, besides, by frequent *crescendi* and *decrescendi*, in accord with the evident sense of the phrases—here indicated with sufficient frequency by the familiar signs ⎯⎯ and ⎯⎯. Where the *crescendo* or *decrescendo* involves more extended passages, however, *cresc.* or *dimin.* has been added. We must also observe, that the earlier virtuosi played with fire and elegance combined, but without greater admixture of their own subjectivity than was unavoidable; for then much less was said about "individual conception" than now-a-days. One hundred years ago, this style of interpretation was termed "modest"—a word which accurately expresses the entire idea. For the rest, our expression-marks can lead to a true interpretation of Bach's piano-pieces only when they are not taken in sharp and sudden contrast, but with smooth transitions, faster or slower according to circumstances, in passing from one to another.

Touching the separate numbers of this volume, the following remarks are offered:

1. Twelve little Preludes for Beginners (page 3).

These pieces were probably jotted down by Bach while he was giving lessons, and were adapted to the immediate needs of individual pupils. Proofs for this assertion are afforded by Nos. 1, 4, 5, 8-11. which were written in the "Clavierbüchlein für W. F. Bach" by his father's own hand, and are exactly reproduced here. The others were in a volume in J. P. Kellner's handwriting. The date of the "Clavierbüchlein" is the approximate date of their composition (1720).

2. Six little Preludes for Beginners (page 14).

These are engraved after Forkel's old edition, published by C. F. Peters.

3. Little two-part Fugue (page 20).

This fugue, which, by the way, is also extant in the shape of a violin duet in a strange hand, appears in the present new edition with some not unessential emendations by J. P. Kellner's hand.

4. Fugue in C-major (page 22).

Reproduced after a single copy in Forkel's literary remains, no other exemplar being obtainable. It was probably written in Cöthen, shortly prior to 1723, as it exhibits the characteristics of the master's sublimest art-period.

5. Fugue in C-major (page 24).

After the autograph from the "Clavierbuchlein" above mentioned. This source approximately establishes the time of its composition. It appears to have been written as an exercise for the two weakest fingers, especially of the right hand.

6. Prelude and Fughetta, in D-minor (page 26).

7. Prelude and Fughetta, in E-minor (page 28).

For these two pieces autographs were at hand, and were followed implicitly. From their style we may conclude that they were written in Cöthen, before 1723.

8. Prelude and Fugue, in A-minor (page 33).

Of this piece only one copy could be found, in J. P. Kellner's hand, who, though himself a fine fugue-writer and a zealous admirer of Bach, was very often a careless copyist. The editor's task was, therefore, confined to the discovery and correction of slips of the pen. It is probable that this piece was written some years earlier than the two preceding.

F. K. GRIEPENKERL

SHORT PRELUDES AND FUGUES

12124

I.
Twelve little Preludes for Beginners.

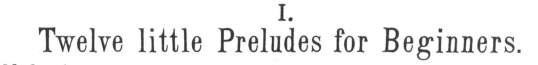

For the convenience of Students, the embellishments are in this Edition written out in full in smaller notes. The following are the principal signs and the manner in which they are to be played. *Ed.*

a.) Mordent; played: b.) Trill with slide from below, and after-beat; played:

c.) Trill with slide from above, and after-beat; played: d.) Inverted Mordent; played:

Printed in the U.S.A.

4

Allegro non troppo.

2.

Allegro con moto.

3.

Andante con moto.

4.

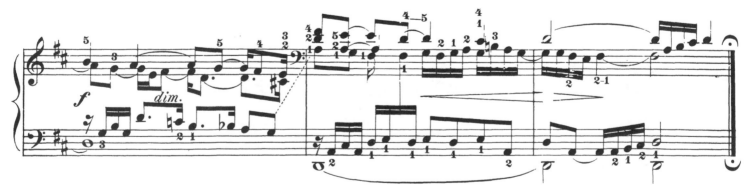

Moderato tranquillo.

5.

Andante espressivo.

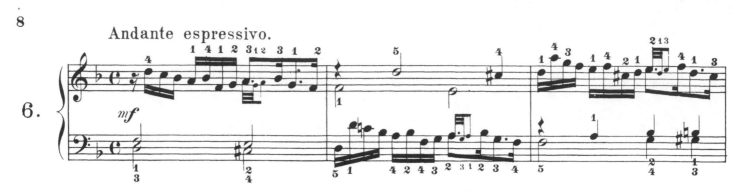

6.

Allegretto.

7.

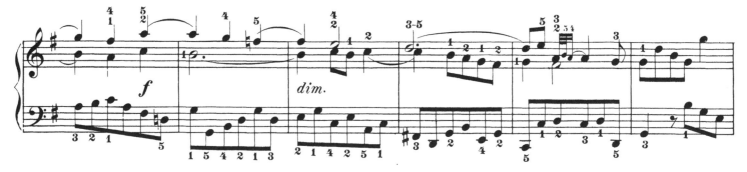

Allegro.

8.

poco a poco dim.

poco riten.

a.) This F, in connection with the F sharp in the bass which immediately precedes it form a false relation. It is found, however, in all the best Editions. *Editor.*

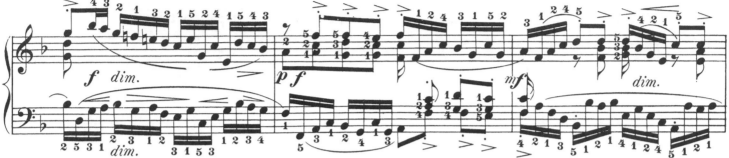

Minuet – Trio.
Allegretto.

10.

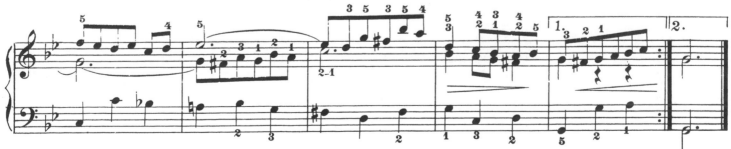

Andantino.

11.

Allegretto.

12.

II.
Six little Preludes for Beginners.

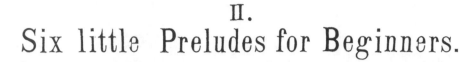

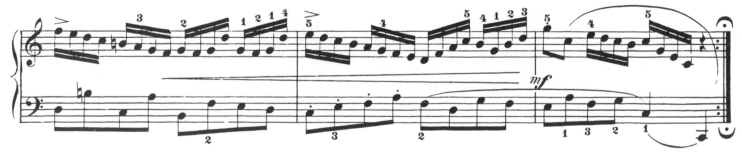

Con moto.

2.

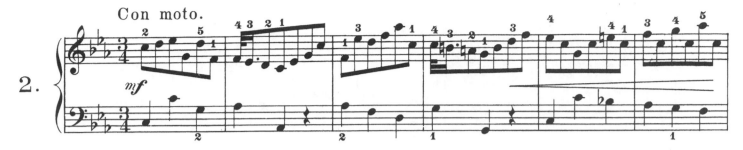

12124

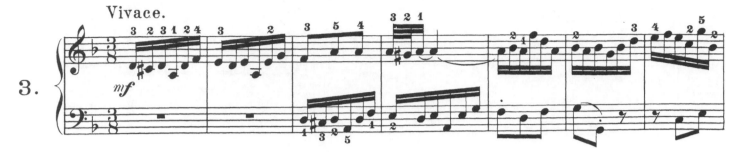

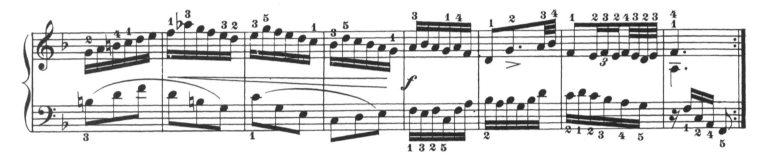

Allegretto grazioso.

4.

non legato.

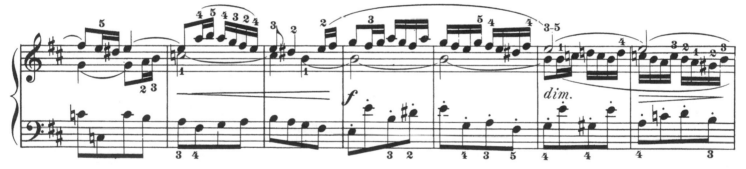

Allegro, ma non troppo.

5.

19

Allegro.

6.

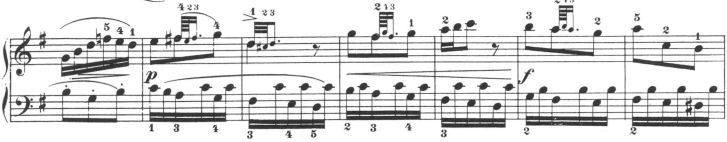

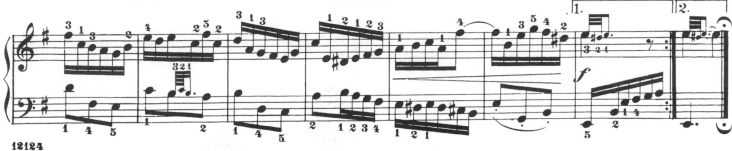

12124

Little two-part Fugue.

III.

a.) etc.

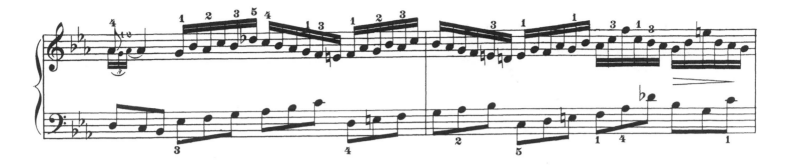

Fugue.

Allegro moderato.

IV.

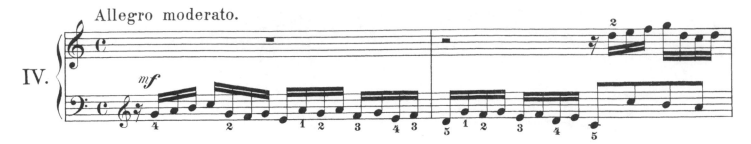

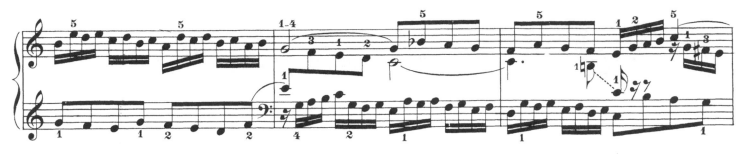

poco a poco cresc.

dim.

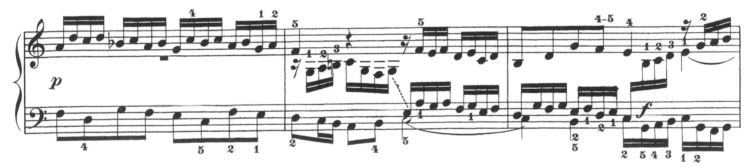

Fugue.

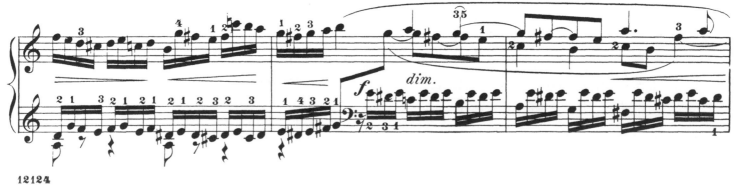

Prelude and Fughetta.

Prelude.
Sostenuto.

VI.

Fughetta.

Andante.

Prelude and Fughetta.

Prelude.
Andantino.

VII.

Fughetta.

Moderato.

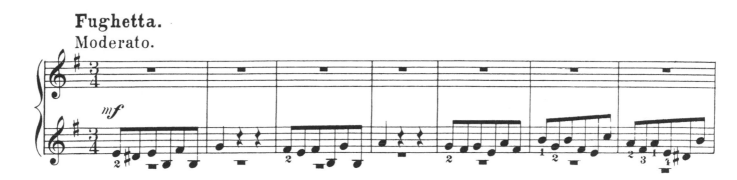

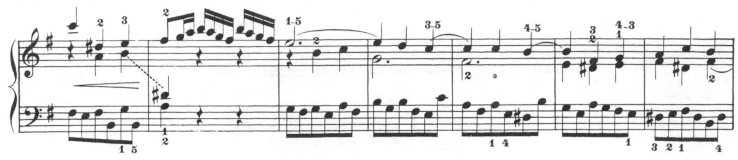

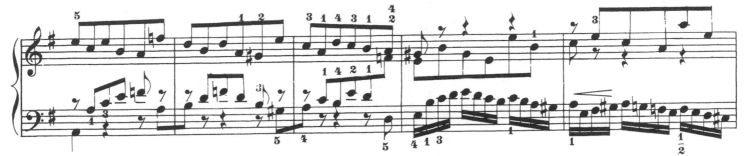

12124

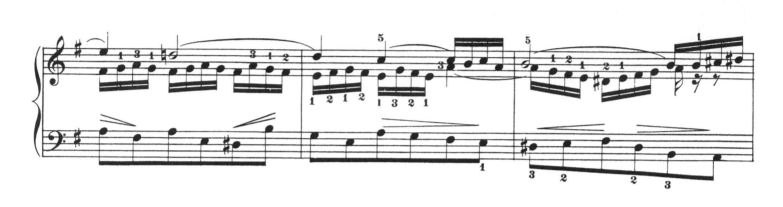

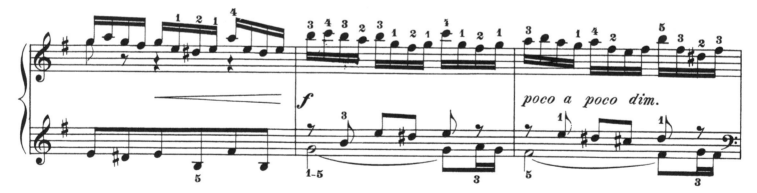

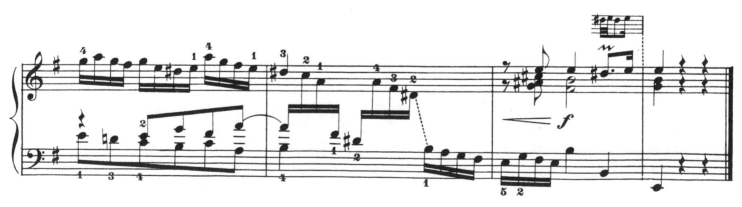

Prelude and Fugue.

Prelude.
Moderato.

VIII.

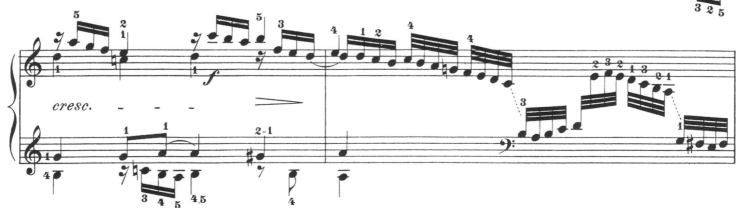

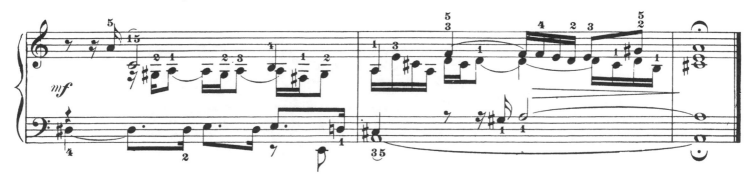

Fugue.
Allegro non troppo.

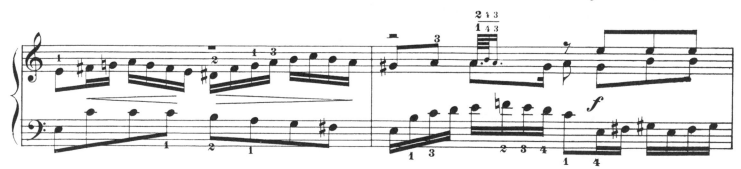